# TRUSTEE HANDBOOK

## SIXTH EDITION

*Barbara Hadley Stanton*

National Association of Independent Schools
1620 L Street NW
Washington, D.C. 20036

**Library of Congress Cataloging-in-Publication Data**
Stanton, Barbara Hadley, 1935–
    Trustee handbook / Barbara Hadley Stanton. — 6th ed.    p.    cm.
    Rev. ed. of: Trustee handbook / Eric W. Johnson. 5th ed.   c1984.
    ISBN 0-934338-70-1
    1. Private school trustees—United States—Handbooks, manuals, etc.
2. Private schools—United States—Administration—Handbooks, manuals, etc.
I. National Association of Independent Schools.   II. Johnson, Eric W. Trustee
handbook.   III. Title.
LB2831.3.S73   1989                                                        89–38170
371'.02—dc20                                                                    CIP

*Tot Wright*

# CONTENTS

# *Contents*

*Contents*

vi

# PREFACE

The *Trustee Handbook* is the all-time best seller among NAIS publications. This is as it should be, for trustees of independent schools hold the key to the long-term well-being of this vital sector of American education. We calculate that there are 15,000 NAIS trustees, of whom 3,000 to 4,000 are new each year. We hope that the *Trustee Handbook* provides a fast and thorough guide of new trustees and a refresher for veterans.

This is officially the sixth edition of the handbook, but it has been so thoroughly rewritten that it is practically a new book. That, too, is as it should be; even in the five years since the fifth edition appeared independent school trusteeship has changed greatly and its responsibilities have increased.

There are new pressures on the independent school: more competition from improving public schools, declining numbers of middle and secondary school children, more complicated government regulations, tax reforms that make giving more expensive, the need for improving faculty compensation, and financial and other relatively recent complexities.

These forces require a much more sophisticated and knowledgeable board. They also make more complicated—and crucial—the leadership of the board and the leadership of the school. Acknowledging this, NAIS is putting more emphasis on serving board chairs and school heads. We see the *Trustee Handbook* not as a reference work for the bookshelf but as a teaching manual for the newly tougher task of trusteeship. We hope especially that it will help in understanding the sensitive and vital relationship between the school head and the board.

We appreciate and honor the work of author Barbara Hadley Stanton, long an independent school stalwart, trustee, board chair, and onetime chair of the NAIS Trustee Committee—comprising a rotating panel of accomplished and experienced trustees—which carries the responsibility for advising on NAIS activities and services in the the area of trusteeship and school governance.

We believe that independent school trustees will be well served by the author's new work and by the guidance of the committee. We commend this book to *all* trustees.

*John C. Esty, Jr.*
*President, NAIS*

# INTRODUCTION

This sixth edition of *The Trustee Handbook*, like the first edition twenty-five years ago, is a guide to the responsibilities and organization of an independent school board. The responsibilities are the same for every school, large or small, but because there are many kinds of independent schools, there are many kinds of successful board organization.

This handbook is intended as a practical resource for boards and heads. The first chapter gives a summary of independent school trusteeship that may aid in the orientation of new trustees. In later chapters, more experienced trustees will find sections on the responsibilities of each of the common standing committees. We hope that board chairs and school heads, seeking to help their boards be wise governors of their schools, will find the handbook generally useful.

The National Association of Independent Schools and its member local, state, and regional associations stand ready to help trustees and heads with information and advice about almost all school situations. These organizations also offer programs for boards, heads, administrators, and faculty members.

The author gratefully acknowledges the permission of the Kellogg Foundation and of Independent Sector to adapt material from, respectively, Cyril C. Houle, *The Effective Board* (New York: The Association Press, 1960), and Kenneth N. Dayton, ''Governance Is Governance,'' an Independent Sector Occasional Paper, published in 1987. (A revision of Cyril Houle's work, entitled *Governing Boards: Their Nature and Nur-*

*ture,* was published in 1989 by Jossey-Bass, San Francisco, and The National Center for Nonprofit Boards, Washington, D.C.)

The statistics in this edition, except where otherwise noted, are drawn from responses to a 1988 stratified sampling of NAIS school heads and board chairs.

Particular thanks are owed to the authors of previous editions of this handbook, to past and present members of the NAIS Trustee Committee, and to the many trustees and heads whose experience and wisdom are reflected in the text.

*Barbara Hadley Stanton*
*Spring 1989*

# 1.

# INDEPENDENT SCHOOL TRUSTEESHIP

The board of an independent school has the ultimate responsibility for the institution. School heads and trustees come and go; only the board is permanent. The board is responsible for the integrity of the school, the standing and reputation built by its founders and by those who have labored over the years. The board holds in trust the school's future as well as its present; the board's collective judgment will affect how the institution can serve constituencies to come. Effective independent school trusteeship is both a deeply challenging and a deeply rewarding endeavor.

Most independent school trustees have ties to the school. They know students and parents and, often, faculty members. As a result, school trusteeship differs from service on other not-for-profit boards, whose trustees may not know clients or staff. Because of the closeness of school communities, school trustees have to be careful to separate trustee decisions from family ones and to act, whenever possible, to support the authority of the head of the school.

The revision of this handbook five times since its original publication testifies to a continuing evolution in the responsibilities of independent schools and their boards. Particularly, there have been changes in the relation between the school and its students and parents and in the relation between the head, the faculty, and the board.

First, many parents new to independent schools need to learn that schools look for parental involvement in their children's education and in volunteer service to the school. Because both parents now usually work—in part to afford independent education—to ask the gift of time is to ask a great deal. Schools and boards need to show why this gift is essential. To do this, they may have to account more fully than in the past concerning the management of the school and the board.

Second, there is a growing sense of partnership within the school: an increasing recognition of the head's need for the board's considered support, of the faculty's need to be informed and have its concerns heard, and of the board's responsibility to assess the effects of school policies and programs. This sense of partnership, which challenges the traditional concept of hierarchical management, calls for new qualities of leadership and trusteeship. Boards and heads must devise forms of board organization that respond to these changing needs and responsibilities in the context of their particular school.

# Five concepts of trusteeship

Five concepts are central to independent school trusteeship: ethos, change, partnership, leadership, and volunteer service.

## Ethos

A school's ethos is its mission and characteristic spirit: its reason for existence. This combination of mission and spirit, of purpose and philosophy, is, above all, what guides a board as it plans educationally and financially, makes policy, and assesses the school's performance. The board's relation to the administration and faculty is as much an expression of the school's ethos as what takes place in the school's classrooms and on its playing fields—and will have as great an effect on the future of the institution.

The concept of ethos is a reminder that a school is not run for tangible profit and that what goes into and comes out of an education is almost certainly beyond measure. While boards must try to measure input and outcome as carefully as they can, and the management of the school must be businesslike, in the last analysis the vital service a school provides is basically unquantifiable.

## Change

The constituencies of a school—students, faculty, administration, parents, graduates, donors, local community, trustees—change to some extent each year, as does the moral, intellectual, and social climate in which the school operates. As a result, schools are always in flux; they cannot rest. The board should expect continual change, try to anticipate it, and use it as an opportunity for the school.

## Partnership

The working relationship between the board, particularly the board chair, and the head of the school is a partnership of mutual endeavor and trust. Legally, the board is responsible for the institution and selects the head to be the educational leader and administrator of the school. The head is a full-time professional, the board is part-time and volunteer, but each has skills, knowledge, resources, and judgment essential to the school. To serve the institution well, they need to work cooperatively and communicate openly in an atmosphere of mutual respect.

The relation between an independent school board and its head is a more even partnership than is the case in other not-for-profit institutions. For instance, in many performing arts organizations the role of the board is almost entirely to raise money to support the vision of the founder or the artistic director. Similarly, in some churches, once the church board selects a new minister, that person becomes the presiding officer of the board as well as the leader of the church: board chair and chief executive officer in one. The responsibilities of an independent school board and head are more balanced and, hence, more interdependent. As a result, situations arise in which board and head may legitimately differ in their interpretation of where authority lies. Understanding and accommodation are needed to make this partnership work for the school.

Defining the responsibilities of board and head is more complicated than the usual distinction between policy and administration. The board sets policy and delegates administration of the school to the head, subject to the board's review. But the head guides the board in setting policy, while the board has primary administrative responsibility for its own management, for managing the school's assets, and for raising money.

## Leadership

The leadership of an independent school is the responsibility of the head and the board chair. The head is the professional leader of the school; the chair is the leader of the board. Both are crucial to the school. They are there to make a difference, to articulate their vision of what the institution can be, and to persuade others to work toward this end. Each trustee has the right to expect leadership from the head and from the chair.

## Volunteer service

Finally, independent school trusteeship requires volunteer service on the board, among the school's constituencies, and in the larger community of those not part of the school. Each trustee takes on the obligation of active support for the school, for the the leadership of the school head, and for independent education.

One component of volunteer service is financial support of the school: each trustee should contribute something to every school fund-raising effort. But volunteer service entails the gift of time and thought and effort as well. Independent schools exist because of volunteer service, one of the concepts embodied in independent education.

# The board's responsibilities

An independent school operates in the public interest. The board has an obligation to hold the school to the highest standards of service to the public from which the school derives its independence. As tax-exempt institutions, independent schools cannot justify their existence if their function is only to provide for those already privileged by society.

An independent school board has four principal responsibilities. Outlined here, they are covered more fully in the chapters that follow.

1. **The board organizes and manages itself so as to fulfill its duties to the school.**
   - ☐ The board establishes a way of working that is compatible with situations that may arise within the school. A school's procedures sustain its people, and, through them, the school. It is often difficult to institute a procedure at the time it is most needed. To do so may imply that things have not been well handled in the past.

It is easier to deal with change if a procedure is already in place and is a routine part of the board's operations.

☐ The board conducts an annual written evaluation to monitor its own performance and the performance of the chair and to set its goals for the coming year.

☐ Trustees are responsible to the institution as a whole. No trustee represents a constituency. Even if elected by a particular group within the school, a trustee does not represent that group on the board.

Only the board as a whole gives direction to the school. Until the full board in a properly constituted meeting decides an issue, even the chair cannot speak for the board.

**2. The board plans, develops and establishes policy, and assesses the performance of the school.**

☐ The board, with the guidance of the head, establishes the school's mission, develops the strategic plan, and formulates general policies. It monitors the administration's progress in carrying out the plan.

☐ The board is involved in developing the school's major internal policy statements and operating procedures.

☐ The board reviews the school's policies and programs to make sure that they are consonant with the school's ethos, effective, and well managed.

**3. The board is responsible for the school's financial condition and its physical plant.**

☐ The board approves the annual operating budget and receives an annual audit or review of the school's financial operations and assets.

☐ The board monitors the school's financial management. It approves capital expenditures above authorized limits.

☐ The board makes sure that the physical plant is adequate for the school's programs.

☐ To ensure that the school has the financial and physical resources it needs, the board bears primary responsibility for the financial stability of the school and for fund raising.

**4. The board selects the head of the school and works cooperatively with that person.**

☐ The search committee of the board, with or without the help of a consultant, defines the qualities needed in the new head and, after gaining the board's approval of this definition, examines and recommends candidates to the board.

☐ The board delegates administration of the school to the head, subject to the board's review.

☐ The board assesses the administration of the school through a yearly written evaluation of the head's performance.

☐ The board has an obligation to support the head's leadership. A trustee who receives a complaint refers the matter promptly to the head so as not to undercut the authority delegated to the head. Except when required by law, the board does not sit as a court of appeal for parents, students, or faculty members concerning the head's actions.

☐ Each trustee helps to keep the school's constituencies informed and is an advocate for the school.

# The head's responsibilities

The head of the school has three major responsibilities.

**1. The head serves as the professional educational leader of the institution.**

☐ The head guides the board in formulating the school's mission and in developing its strategic plan.

☐ The head articulates the mission of the school to its constituencies.

☐ The head is responsible for the professional quality and behavior of the faculty.

**2. The head administers the school according to the policies set by the board.**

☐ The head prepares and carries out the operating plan and the annual budget.

☐ The head has complete responsibility for faculty, staff, and student selection, evaluation, and dismissal.

❏ The head has the duty to report to the board on school matters. The head is accountable to the board for effective, businesslike management of the institution.

3. **The head works with the chair to enable the board to carry out its responsibilities.**

❏ Head and chair jointly plan the board calendar for the year, draw up the agendas of board meetings, and make arrangements for keeping each trustee and each constituency informed about the school.

# The board chair's responsibilities

The board chair also has three main responsibilities.

1. **The chair is the administrative leader of the board.**

❏ The chair makes sure that the board fulfills its responsibilities to the school. The effectiveness of a board depends on its chair.

❏ The chair, with the head, decides the issues to be dealt with by the board and sets board agendas.

❏ The chair expedites the work of the board and keeps board committees on schedule.

2. **The chair works in partnership with the head to achieve the mission of the school.**

❏ The chair and the head lead the institution. They counsel, criticize, and encourage each other in this demanding, frustrating, but often joyful enterprise.

❏ The chair and head speak for the school to its constituencies.

3. **The chair is responsible for the working relations between board and head.**

❏ The chair devises a way of working for the board that complements the strengths and weaknesses of the head.

❏ The chair conducts the board's annual evaluation of the head and reports the responses to the head and to the board.

❏ The chair, working with the committee on trustees, makes sure that the board conducts an annual written evaluation of its performance and that of the chair.

❑ The chair serves as an example of trusteeship to less experienced trustees.

These respective responsibilities of board, head, and board chair are fairly simple in theory but are more than occasionally ambiguous and complicated in fact. One complication is that in schools, as in religious organizations, even routine decisions are expressions of the ethos of the institution. As a result, almost all matters can be interpreted as involving both educational policy and school administration. Boards and heads each therefore may have reason to feel that the authority rests with them.

A second complication is that schools are composed of individuals having individual strengths and vulnerabilities. Institutions have to adjust somewhat to the people in charge.

A third complication is that procedures for board-head communication, for regular evaluations, and for responding to complaints are often allowed to lapse.

These procedures, along with a shared sense of school goals, a willingness to listen to other points of view, trust, and discretion are essential to sound working relations between board and head.

## Additional resources

Dayton, Kenneth N. "Governance Is Governance." Independent Sector Occasional Paper. Independent Sector, 1828 L St. N.W., Washington, D.C. 20036. 1987.

Houle, Cyril O. *Governing Boards: Their Nature and Nurture.* San Francisco: Jossey-Bass, 1989.

# 2.

# BOARD
# SELF-MANAGEMENT

The board is responsible for organizing and managing itself to fulfill its duties to the school. The board chair is in charge of this process, assisted and monitored by the committee on trustees. (For the responsibilities of this committee, also called the nominating committee, see page 14.)

Board responsibilities are the same in all schools but can be met in different ways. An institution's ethos, size, type (elementary, secondary, boarding, day), and stage of development all affect how its board may operate best. Each board needs to devise a way of working appropriate to its school. As the school and its leadership change, the board may want to adjust its way of working.

Trusteeship requires the gift of time, which is usually in short supply. Trustee time should be spent on essential board responsibilities; much should be delegated to the head and the administration. A board needs to control its time demands so that trustees can afford to serve the school for more than a few years.

In the 1970's the accounting and consulting firm of Touche Ross studied trustee time commitments in efficient not-for-profit boards. Barring emergencies, roughly half the trustees gave an average of five to ten hours a month, a quarter gave eleven to twenty hours a month, and another quarter gave more than twenty hours. More recent figures compiled by Korn Ferry International and Heidrick & Struggles, two other consulting firms, indicate similar commitments for outside directors of corporate boards. In 1987 these directors devoted an average of 111 hours annually —about ten hours a month—to board matters.

For independent school boards, these averages probably should apply only during the months school is in session. They should include time spent on everything involved in being a trustee: school visits, telephone calls, preparing for meetings, attending committee and board meetings, and attending formal and informal functions connected with the school.

The Touche Ross study suggests a way of analyzing the self-management of independent school boards. If most trustees are putting in an average of more than ten hours a month during the school year, the board may not be delegating enough. Conversely, if only the chair is contributing more than twenty hours a month, the board may not be working as hard as the school needs it to. Board chairs of NAIS member schools average about forty hours a month on school business when school is in session.

# Board organization

The school's *charter* from the state describes its purpose and makes the board accountable for the institution. Supporting the charter are written *bylaws,* which set board size and procedures. Unlike the charter, which can be changed only by state action, bylaws can be amended by the board at any time to reflect current school needs.

*Minutes* provide a record of board and committee decisions and are evidence that the board is acting in accordance with the school's charter and all applicable federal, state, and local laws.

A board *policy book,* kept up to date by the secretary, is useful for reference and in trustee orientation. A policy book includes excerpts from the minutes classified by topic, such as school mission and goals, admission and financial aid policies, finance and budgeting procedures, and staffing and personnel policies. The book may also describe matters that do and do not require board approval, how the head should report administrative implementation of actions taken by the board, and procedures for proposing policy changes.

- ☐ The charter and bylaws should be reviewed periodically by a lawyer to make sure they reflect actual practice. Further, school policies should be reviewed annually to be sure that they conform to current state and federal laws and regulations.
- ☐ Under law, schools are required to keep a record of board minutes, and, in some states, also of committee minutes.
- ☐ Board members need to be aware of their legal obligations and of the board's procedures for avoiding trustee conflict of interest.

## Officers

The bylaws specify the officers of the board: generally a *board chair, treasurer* (or chair of the finance committee), and *secretary.* A board may wish also to designate a *vice chair;* some states mandate it.

The duties of the chair and treasurer are described below in the sections dealing with their responsibilities (chair, pp. 7 and 51; treasurer, pp. 34 and 43.) Officers are nominated yearly by the committee on trustees. If possible, the chair and treasurer should agree to serve for at least three years; both board and head need this continuity of experience, leadership, and counsel.

The selection of a new board chair or treasurer can be a delicate matter if the preferred candidate feels unable to serve. When this happens, the board must unite behind a second or third choice—without the board or final candidate being aware of this process. To avoid embarrassment, the incumbent chair usually sounds trustees out individually and approaches a candidate informally before official nomination by the committee on trustees.

- ☐ The committee should make sure that the nominee for board chair is acceptable to the head, for they must be able to work together.
- ☐ It is good practice to try to have two potential replacements on the board for the offices of chair and treasurer.
- ☐ If at all possible, officers should have been trustees for at least two years. Otherwise, they lack both knowledge and credibility.
- ☐ It is seldom advisable to ask former officers to continue to serve on the board after their terms end. Even though they are removed from the center of power, their presence may inhibit new officers from making necessary changes.

The *secretary* gives the trustees advance notice of meetings as prescribed in the bylaws, keeps the board minutes and policy book, and is usually the custodian of the institution's seal (necessary for legal documents). If the secretary feels unable to take notes while participating in discussions, the board may designate a nontrustee, such as the head's secretary, the business manager, or the development director, to be secretary. This person must be as discreet as a trustee.

## Committees

Almost all boards operate at least partially through committees, but the number of committees and how they are used varies greatly. A committee has the advantage of specialization: it can study a complicated situation in depth and bring carefully thought-out proposals to the board. At the same time, decisions may be improved by the involvement of other trustees, and only the full board has the power to make major decisions. Each board has to find its own balance between committee specialization and board involvement.

A committee studies a particular matter (such as athletics or faculty compensation), an area of school operation (student life, the educational program), or is responsible for a board administrative function (trustees, finance, development).

Standing committees have a continuing duty to review and deal with matters that the board faces each year. Ad hoc committees are formed as need arises to deal with less frequently recurring issues (such as the school's public relations program or tuition remission policy for faculty children). Most school programs and operations may be studied either by a standing committee or an ad hoc committee. Board administrative responsibilities generally are better carried out by standing committees.

The usual standing committees, listed below, may be called by other names. Few schools have all of them, some probably have more than they need, and others manage quite well with only two or three from this list. Committee responsibilities are described in the sections covering the board responsibilities they undertake.

☐ Committee on trustees (p. 14)

☐ Executive committee (p. 15)

Two additional committees, although not standing committees, are included among the usual ones: the search committee (p. 61), and the head's advisory committee (p. 66).

## Organizing and running committees

The following are guidelines for forming, organizing, and managing committees.

**1.** A committee is advisable when specialization can produce better decision making or management, or when personal involvement is likely to create ownership.

**2.** Committees report to the board and exercise only those powers delegated to them by the board. The board chair, with the advice of the head and the board, sets the yearly goals for each committee.

**3.** The head and chair are members of all committees ex officio (by virtue of their office), though they may choose not to attend all meetings.

**4.** Each committee has a written charge, a schedule of reporting to the board, or a deadline for making recommendations to the board.

**5.** A committee's size depends on its charge. Four or five members, including the chair and the head, usually is sufficient for the committee on trustees. A total of six to eight members is plenty for most tasks. Nine or more members tends to be unwieldy but is advisable in strategic planning for reasons of inclusiveness and ownership.

**6.** A committee recommending action to the board prepares a written report sent in advance of the board meeting. The report states the problem, the alternatives considered, the committee's recommendations, and what these recommendations may entail for the budget, plant use, faculty and staff time, and public relations. The report should be as brief as possible.

**7.** A committee recommendation need not be accepted by the board but can serve as the basis for board discussion of the matter.

**8.** The board chair or the head—preferably the chair—works closely with committee chairs to keep things moving.

**9.** Committees need secretarial help in sending out meeting reminders, agendas, and minutes. This help sometimes comes from the school but in many cases needs to be supplied by a trustee.

**10.** Committee members are appointed yearly by the board on the recommendation of the committee on trustees or the board chair. If possible, every trustee should serve on at least one committee. Some trustees should be new to each standing committee each year.

## The committee on trustees

The nominating committee, when it is functioning properly, is the most important board committee because it oversees the quality of the board and the board's self-management. Since the scope of this committee includes far more than nominations, NAIS suggests that its title be the *committee on trustees.* It should be a standing committee composed of a few experienced and respected current trustees (for it is almost impossible for former trustees to know the board's current needs). The committee should be representative of the board; a committee consisting only of three or four of the board's most senior members, for example, would appear to deny itself the perspective of younger members. The board chair and the head serve as active ex officio members.

A fully functioning committee on trustees has six responsibilities.

**1.** The committee measures the board's formal and informal organization yearly against the requirements of the strategic plan and the board's previous evaluation.

**2.** The committee works closely with the board chair, advising and aiding in board management, such as determining other committee assignments or planning retreats.

**3.** To the extent that the board perpetuates itself, the committee selects and nominates candidates for the board. (See trustee selection and nomination, p. 21).

**4.** The committee nominates board officers and the members and heads of all committees other than itself. The committee on trustees and its chair are nominated by the board chair.

**5.** The committee works with the board chair to establish and oversee the trustee orientation process.

**6.** The committee conducts the yearly board and board chair evaluation and reports responses to the board.

## The executive committee

The executive committee, where one exists, is a small group of experienced trustees, usually the officers of the board and the chairs of major committees. The executive committee may have a wide range of responsibilities. In addition to making decisions delegated to it by the board between board meetings, it may advise the head and the board chair, evaluate the head, monitor the progress of the operating plan, and, in the absence of a finance committee, approve the budget before it is presented to the board. It may also conduct the search for a new head. The executive committee, like any committee, acts within limits set by the board and reports any action at the board's next meeting.

If there is an executive committee, it should take care not to become a superboard or a policy-making group in itself. The danger of its taking on this function and becoming *the* committee to be on is one reason why many boards have no executive committee. There is no surer way to kill trustee interest than to have the executive committee do most of the board's planning and thinking. It will soon divide the board into first- and second-class citizens.

## Board size

The boards of most NAIS schools have between fifteen and twenty-five members. According to the management consulting firm of Spencer Stuart and Associates, major corporate boards in 1987 ranged in size from eight to twenty-seven directors, with a median of fourteen.

Independent school boards probably need to be somewhat larger than corporate boards; unlike corporate directors, some trustees usually have to be actively involved in fund raising. As a result, unless a school can afford extensive staff support, fewer than fifteen trustees is seldom enough to fulfill an independent school board's responsibilities.

However, a board also needs to be small enough to function as a unified group for purposes of discussion and decision making; this is difficult with twenty-five members. When a board gets too large, a smaller in-group, such as an executive committee, often begins to make most of the decisions, with the consequences described above.

In place of having a large board, nontrustees can be asked to serve on selected board committees. This practice allows boards to keep to a manageable size and to see potential trustees in action. Whatever their composition, committees should be chaired, or cochaired, by a trustee, and trustees should ordinarily constitute a majority of any committee.

## Board composition

A school needs thoughtful, dedicated trustees who fit the board's and the school's needs, are prepared to volunteer sufficient time to learn about the school and about trusteeship, and come prepared to board and committee meetings. Trustees must be discreet, for board discussions are absolutely confidential. Lack of confidentiality is a breach of trust, which can damage a school severely.

Trustees are responsible to the institution as a whole. No trustee should formally represent a particular constituency. For example, if the head of the parents' association or the graduates' association is a trustee ex officio, that person, as a trustee, does not represent the parents or the graduate body.

Similarly, trustees who are parents of children in the school should be able to decide an issue for the good of the school, not just for the good of their children. During board deliberations, each trustee decides for the good of the entire school.

Over 85 percent of NAIS *school heads* serve as members of the board ex officio or as full trustees. Whether they are trustees or not, heads receive notice of and attend all board meetings and receive copies of all board and board committee minutes.

If a board has reason to meet in executive session without the head, the chair should tell the head about the impending session and its purpose as far ahead of time as possible and, immediately after the meeting, report any action taken. A head has the right to know the gist of what has been said in any executive session. Executive sessions are necessary in extreme circumstances when the board is considering whether to request the head's resignation, but otherwise they should be rare indeed; they destroy the trust between board and head by implying that there is information that the head should not have.

Approximately 15 percent of NAIS member schools have *faculty members* serving as full trustees. An additional 38 percent have faculty observers at board meetings, and 66 percent have teachers as members of selected board committees. Like all trustees, faculty members who are trustees do not represent a constituency and should be able to decide for the good of the school even if this may adversely affect colleagues.

In many states trustees must be at least eighteen years old. Perhaps, as a result, only about 2 percent of NAIS schools have *students* as trustees, and only about 6 percent have student observers at board meetings. Most of these boards limit student participation to service on a few committees, such as strategic planning or head search.

A board needs diversity of people and talents. Business and financial skills are needed, but many others are equally essential. Among them are architecture, arts, construction, communications, community organization, politics, and real estate. Boards can lead by introducing greater gender, ethnic, and multicultural diversity, either from within the school or from the outside community.

The head of another school that does not compete directly can bring perspective to a board, as can members of the clergy, people from the community where the school is located, representatives of higher education, and other people interested in the school but external to it. It is better if such trustees do not have close pre-existing friendships with the head.

Only a few trustees will or should be wealthy. One formula states, "Of work, wealth, and wisdom, a trustee should contribute at least two." Those who are willing to contribute only wealth might be asked to become members of a donors' council that meets yearly to receive a briefing on the school and is called upon occasionally for contacts or fund raising. It is demoralizing for other trustees if a few wealthy board members do no work and attend no meetings, and wealthy potential trustees are quick to note that service on such a board is no honor.

## Trustee tenure

Boards need to concern themselves with regular turnover and selective tenure. They should have a working rotation policy that brings in enthusiastic new trustees with fresh points of view and makes possible the retirement of unproductive board members. At the same time, the continuity and perspective provided by a limited number of dedicated long-term trustees is extremely valuable.

In the 1960's, some boards had no effective provision for rotation or board evaluation. Even though these boards were experienced, events of the late 1960's and early 1970's often proved them to be thoroughly out of touch with their schools' constituencies. In reaction, more than 45 percent of NAIS member schools (generally day schools) now permit only two three-year terms of trustee service before a mandatory year off, with no extension for board officers.

Unfortunately, this six-year limit to trustee service also has proved unsatisfactory. Effective trustees have to retire at the height of their usefulness, the large yearly influx of new trustees impedes board functioning, and heads soon find themselves with no trustees from the board that gave them their original mandate. While most boards allow former trustees to return to the board after a year and to serve on board committees in the interim, almost all former trustees, feeling that they have done their bit, do not return.

In trying to combine turnover with tenure, some bylaws provide for two four- or five-year terms before a mandatory year off the board. But even four years is a long time to suffer an unproductive trustee. Other possible approaches include the following two alternatives. Any board interested in either one should consult a lawyer to make sure that its provisions are allowed by the state in which the school operates.

**1.** Board officers or chairs of major board committees are exempt from rotation either for the period they hold board or committee office or until their latest trustee term expires. Often a maximum is set—nine to twelve years—for the number of consecutive years any trustee can serve.

**2.** The board has two classes of trustees. One class may be re-elected for a maximum of two or three terms and then must leave the board for a year. In addition, a quarter to a third of the total board seats are reserved for a second class of trustees, "corporate" or "school" members, who have proved their worth as trustees and are elected to serve without specific term. In this case a retirement age often is set.

## Board meetings

Boarding school trustees usually come together three or four times a year, holding committee meetings in the afternoon and board meetings in the evening and the following morning. However, approximately 55 percent of NAIS day school boards meet eight or more times a year. This frequency places a heavy burden on the board—especially on the chair, who must spend a good deal of time preparing for meetings and following up after them. This combination of frequent meetings and rapid trustee rotation has resulted in a very brief tenure for many day school board chairs.

In NAIS day schools, 58 percent of the current chairs have held office for less than two years, as compared with 25 percent of the boarding school chairs. The median term of service for day school chairs is a little less than two years; for boarding school chairs it is a little under five years. Two years is seldom long enough for a chair to establish leadership. As a result, many day school boards lose the advantages of continuity, their schools lose potential leadership, and their heads lose informed support.

There may be temporary circumstances under which an independent school board needs to meet eight or more times a year. A board that routinely meets this often, however, probably is not delegating enough authority to the head or is not organizing itself adequately. Well-organized day school boards usually need to meet no more than five or six times a year for an hour and a half or two hours at a time. Time taken by additional meetings may deter trustees from further service to the school.

Here are some suggestions for organizing, running, and following up on board meetings.

☐ Board meeting dates should be established ahead for each school year.

☐ If possible, meetings should be at the school so that trustees can see the plant even if the school is closed.

❑ The agenda, the minutes of the previous meeting, and written reports from the head, chair, and pertinent committees should be sent to the trustees ten days before each meeting. The written materials, used for reference and as a basis for discussion, are not read aloud at the meeting. (See the head's duty to report, p. 44.)

❑ Meetings should begin on time. Trustees will arrive promptly when they can count on starting promptly. Many boards also fix a time for ending meetings. Some day schools hold early-morning meetings that adjourn by 9:15.

❑ At the end of each meeting, a five-minute review of what was decided and what went well or badly can help to sum up, allocate tasks, and assess general board functioning.

## Informal board organization

Each board is a social unit with its own culture. The informal ways in which a board functions can be as important as the formal ones. How a board works as a group and its collective attitude toward different personal and management styles affect the quality of its decision making.

Trustees should feel able to speak—and even to admit ignorance—during meetings, not just afterward. They should feel they can talk with the board chair and the head at any time. If this is not the case, trustees should mention their difficulties in the board evaluation, and the committee on trustees should consider how to improve the situation.

A reception, picnic, or barbecue for trustees and spouses can help trustees to feel more at ease with one another. A retreat for the board and senior faculty, or a day when parents, faculty, and trustees together help fix up the school, can foster a sense of trustee and school community.

# Trustee selection, orientation, and evaluation

The committee on trustees is usually responsible for the selection of new trustees and is always in charge of trustee orientation and of board and board chair evaluation. This committee is the most important board committee. The quality of a board can be lost quickly and take years to reestablish. The board needs a steady supply of interested new trustees, trustees need continuing orientation, and the chair and the head need the support of annual evaluations. Once a routine is neglected, reinstituting it becomes an issue—a criticism, open or implied, of what went before. It is better for the school and for all concerned if these procedures remain in regular use.

## Trustee selection and nomination

To the extent that the board is self-perpetuating, selection and nomination of candidates is the responsibility of the committee on trustees, with the active participation of the head and the board chair. Identification and nomination of potential and new trustees, functions that are vital to the future of an institution, are appropriately influenced by perspectives developed from the evaluation of current trustees.

☐ The committee on trustees should consider candidates year-round and make an effort to reach outside the circle of acquaintance of those currently on the board. (See the committee on trustees, p. 14, and board composition, p. 16.)

☐ The committee should be composed of experienced current trustees, because even the most experienced former trustees are unlikely to know present board requirements.

☐ The committee should reflect the composition of the board and include trustees who bring to it a variety of different perspectives. If possible, it should have members closely affiliated to constituences from which the board hopes to recruit.

The evaluation, selection, and nominating process can be summarized in six steps.

**1.** The committee on trustees examines the work and commitment of each current trustee. The committee should be prepared to tell trustees who have missed several meetings or who have not participated as fully as hoped that unless they can make a more active commitment they should make way for others.

**2.** The committee considers what the board has to accomplish in the next few years, which trustees will be rotating off the board, and what skills will be needed. The committee ranks the board's needs in order of importance—business experience, community stature, construction experience, fund-raising ability, and legal expertise, for example. Other committee considerations might include a balance of professional skills, which officers need to be replaced, whether ethnic or cultural diversity and the age range of trustees are consonant with the board's objectives, and whether there is a satisfactory balance on the board of women and men, of parent and graduate trustees, and, in boarding schools, of geographic distribution.

**3.** The committee solicits suggestions for candidates on the basis of projected needs. In addition to the head and the chair, other good sources of names are board members, the director of development, heads of the graduates' and parents' associations, senior faculty members, and former trustees. And, if nontrustees have been serving on board or school committees, their names should automatically be reviewed by the committee on trustees as potential candidates. A form on which to record basic information about candidates, including the names of sponsors and reasons for deferral, is helpful. The committee can keep forms from year to year as a slate of potential candidates.

**4.** The committee makes a preliminary list and asks trustees individually for comments on each candidate. The head asks senior faculty members and administrators for their reactions.

**5.** The committee draws up a final slate and recommends it to the board for approval. The committee should select the people it wants even if the chances of their accepting are not high. They may be able to suggest other names or be willing to serve on an advisory committee. At the least, they will be pleased to have been asked and will have learned something more about the school. The committee nominates new trustees each year, even when no candidates seem exceptionally qualified. It is impossible to tell with certainty in advance which candidates will make the best trustees. (Candidates usually are nominated by yearly "classes" but can be elected at any time.)

**6.** After the board has given its assent, either directly or subject to candidates' accepting nomination, the board chair meets privately with each candidate. The chair should be prepared to speak frankly about the responsibilities of trusteeship, the school's goals, strengths and weaknesses, committees on which the candidate may serve, and expected contributions, in a mutual exploration of the school's needs and the nominee's capabilities, interests, and resources. In doing this, the chair may wish to discuss total trustee giving and the median trustee gift. While each trustee should be expected to make annual contributions to the school, those elected for work and wisdom should not be made to feel that they must also provide wealth by giving beyond their means. However, the chair should withdraw the invitation to join the board if a candidate makes acceptance conditional on not contributing or taking part in fund raising. Trustees cannot arbitrarily excuse themselves from the work of the board.

## Orienting new trustees

Orientation of new trustees takes place before their first board meeting. While the committee on trustees does not conduct the orientation, it coordinates and oversees the process and is responsible for its content. The goal is to have knowledgeable and effective trustees as soon as possible.

- ☐ Faculty trustees should receive the same orientation as other trustees.
- ☐ The heads of the parents' and graduates' associations are among the most important liaisons between the school and its constituencies. Whether they are board members or not, the school would be wise to give them a full orientation.
- ☐ Each new trustee may be assigned a more senior trustee as mentor—someone to turn to with questions during the first year.

The orientation of new trustees can be summarized in four parts.

**1.** The new trustee receives school materials that include the following.

- ☐ Board documents: the school's mission statement, strategic plan, most recent outside evaluation, bylaws, board policy book, minutes of the previous year's meetings with budget projections and comparisons, a list of trustee addresses and telephone numbers, this *Trustee Handbook*

☐ School publications and publicity pieces: the catalogue, sample admission letters, recent press releases, fund-raising appeals

☐ School operations documents: the curriculum, organization chart, faculty and parent directories, a list of student, parent, and faculty committees, building plan or campus map

**2.** New trustees spend at least half a day at the school. They tour the plant—including locker rooms and boiler room—visit classes, meet with senior faculty members and department heads, and learn about admission and financial aid policies, reporting procedures, and student activities.

**3.** The treasurer, board development committee chair, and development director (or other person in charge of development) brief new trustees about the school's financial condition, management, and development program.

**4.** Finally, each new trustee meets separately with the head and with the board chair to discuss the school's goals and the trustee's concerns about the school. The chair takes this occasion to reiterate the responsibilities of trusteeship.

## Continuing trustee orientation

Even experienced trustees need continuing orientation, as follows.

☐ Information from NAIS and its member state, regional, and local associations about developments in legislation and regulations affecting schools. The head or an interested trustee usually is responsible for keeping the board informed about these topics.

☐ New materials developed for the school's constituencies.

☐ An annual visit to school classes. Visits can take place on a regular trustee visiting day or be individually scheduled (on a sign-up sheet passed around at a board meeting). These visits also make trustees visible to the faculty and students, who otherwise might not know what a trustee looks like.

☐ An annual private meeting, with the board chair or with the head, to discuss school concerns.

☐ Attendance at trustee workshops and conferences and, if possible, visits to other schools.

## Board and chair evaluation

Evaluation of the board and board chair are the only institutional procedures through which individual trustees and the head of the school can make suggestions for improving board performance. It is best when these evaluations take the form of an annual written exercise—a normal part of the board's operations.

Some boards fear that evaluation will drive away valuable trustees. This rarely happens; usually trustees welcome the chance to establish more productive ways of working. An evaluation assesses performance, not people.

In this evaluation, trustees examine the board's and the chair's performance and set goals for the coming year. Yearly evaluation allows potential problems to be dealt with routinely, before molehills become mountains. It provides a way of registering progress, and it helps concentrate the attention of the board on the basic mission of the school.

The committee on trustees conducts the board and chair evaluation, which precedes the board's evaluation of the head of the school (see p. 49). The board should make sure its own house is in order before considering the head's performance. This evaluation process usually takes place in the spring and includes the following six steps. (See the Appendix for sample board and chair evaluation forms.)

**1.** The committee on trustees, the board chair, and the head of the school jointly decide on an evaluation process and questionnaire. Deciding what to consider and what format to use is an important part of the evaluation. The evaluation should include a look at how the informal interactions of the trustees with one another and with the head, the board chair, and the faculty may either help or impede board performance. In this context, the committee may decide to ask selected faculty members how they view the board's performance.

**2.** Once the board has reviewed and approved the proposed evaluation process, the committee chair sends the questionnaire to each trustee and to the school head. Respondents need to sign their names because they should be willing to stand behind their opinions and because some people usually need to be reminded to return their questionnaires. However, there should be a clear understanding, to which the board has agreed, about confidentiality or attribution—whether or not the names of individuals may be given—when the responses are discussed with the board chair and the head.

**3.** The committee chair discusses the responses confidentially with the board chair and head.

**4.** The committee chair presents a written summary of responses with recommendations to the board. This summary omits the names of individuals but should make it clear when an opinion is widely held.

**5.** After discussion, the board decides on its goals for the coming year. These in turn serve as the basis of the next year's evaluation. In the process, most boards discover how hard it is to accomplish all they intend.

**6.** The board reviews its procedures for evaluating itself and approves a format for the following year.

## Trustee retirement

When trustees retire from the board, for whatever reason, they should be publicly thanked for their commitment and service. This recognition shows the school's gratitude as well as its appreciation for volunteer service in general.

Some schools have an informal organization of all former trustees (and their spouses) that meets yearly for a reunion and a briefing by the head and board chair. Others have a trustee emeritus status for former trustees who have given especially distinguished service.

### Additional resources

Johnson, Eric W. *Evaluating the Performance of Trustees and School Heads.* Boston: NAIS, 1986.

Saalfield, Albrecht. *A Legal Primer for Independent Schools.* Boston: NAIS, 1983.

# 3

# THE BOARD
# AND THE SCHOOL

The board is responsible for the school and for the welfare of students and faculty. To fulfill this responsibility, the board establishes the school's mission, formulates broad policy, and assesses the performance of the school. The board is responsible for the school's financial condition and for its plant. To ensure that the school has adequate financial and physical resources to carry out its mission, the board bears primary responsibility for fund raising.

## The board and the faculty

The faculty is the heart of the school, and faculty attitudes have a strong bearing on the school's well-being. The board, the administration, and the faculty share a commitment to the institution's mission as a learning community.

As for the welfare of faculty, administration, and staff, the board, through its review process, must ensure that policies on hiring, evaluation, grievances, and dismissal are fair and effective and reflect applicable laws and regulations. Through its financial management, the board does all it can to ensure competitive faculty compensation and to assist the professional development of teachers and administrators.

Professional development can be fostered by providing grants for study, travel, attendance at workshops and conferences, exchange teaching, and sabbatical leave. In 1988, one boarding school allocated just under 2 percent of its budget for these purposes. While this percentage is high, any funds devoted to professional development have an impact far beyond their size on faculty innovation and satisfaction. Unfortunately, these funds are almost always the first to be cut when a school faces budgetary difficulties.

The board's responsibility to the faculty includes a duty to report to the faculty and to provide institutional ways for teachers to make their concerns and opinions known to the board.

Faculty members should be informed promptly about the outcome of board deliberations that affect them and should be able to feel confident that the board is aware of their concerns: The head usually reports pertinent nonconfidential board decisions at the faculty meeting that follows each board meeting.

Most information about faculty concerns and opinions comes to the board through the head. However, as a part of its responsibility to the school and to the faculty, the board needs to be able to assure itself periodically that the head's information is reasonably accurate. For the board to do so is in the head's interest, for if the head is unaware of faculty opinion, the school—and the head—suffer. Schools use a variety of formal and informal arrangements to achieve this goal (joint faculty-trustee committees, for example). It is of paramount importance that any such arrangement be complementary to the board-head relationship, that the head feel secure and included, and that there be no endorsement of structures that facilitate "end runs" around the head.

In a few instances where a head has disregarded or misrepresented faculty concerns, faculties have formed unions to make their case to their boards. Almost always, when communication was re-established, these same faculties have voted the unions out. Such instances underline the responsibility of the board to the faculty. When a board has an accurate sense of a school feeling, it and the head can work together to respond as the situation may require.

Nonetheless, direct board-faculty communication is bound to be disquieting to many heads, for it threatens to circumvent their authority.

28

It is important for this legitimate concern of heads to be recognized. The head should have a voice in formulating the procedures for board-faculty communication and should be fully informed of the process and its outcomes. Whatever procedures are agreed to should be carefully spelled out and followed.

Faculty trusteeship is one institutional method for bringing the opinions and concerns of individual faculty members to board deliberations. Another way, more common, is to have faculty members on selected committees or present as observers at board meetings. (See board composition, p. 16.) A third way is faculty participation in parts of board, board chair, and head evaluations.

- ❑ In all communications with the board, faculty members express their own opinion and do not represent the faculty as a whole.
- ❑ If faculty members are asked to take part in a portion of the evaluation of the head, the board chair should report the gist of these responses promptly, but anonymously, to the head as well as to the board.
- ❑ Neither the board nor a group of trustees should ever meet with faculty delegations. If it did, the board would be acting as a board of appeal concerning particular actions of the head. As a result, even if the board unanimously supported the head, the head's credibility with the faculty would be gravely undermined. The alternatives suggested above are far less disruptive and more informative methods of learning individual faculty concerns. (See also responding to complaints, p. 55.)
- ❑ Some cases of faculty dissatisfaction with the head may result from the head's implementation of board policies. In these cases, responsibility for the head's action—and the faculty's reaction—rests with the board. A board wishing to make changes in a school should consider in advance whether it is prepared to stand behind the head when an unfavorable reaction occurs.

# Planning and realizing the plan

Change will take place without planning, but unplanned change is not always in the best interests of an institution. The object of planning is to identify those changes that may affect an institution and to examine how it might respond.

Planning has two equal components: the strategic plan and the operating plan. With the guidance of the head of the school, the board

- ☐ Establishes the school's mission
- ☐ Determines the strategic plan
- ☐ Makes the policy decisions needed for implementing the plan
- ☐ Monitors the administration's progress toward achieving these goals through the annual operating plan

Planning and policy making are the responsibility of the entire board, but many schools designate a strategic planning committee to make recommendations to the full board.

A strategic plan is developed perhaps every ten years. It is updated, from year to year, in between. The school's operation always should be guided by a current strategic plan. Then capital or annual fund raising or a head search can be undertaken with some assurance that everyone knows where the institution is trying to go.

- ☐ A school should not plan during an emergency, for the exercise will center around the emergency and render any planning ineffective.
- ☐ The planning process should not be used to carry out a hidden agenda. If there is dissatisfaction with the effectiveness of the head or board chair, that situation should be addressed independently, and preferably prior to, a long-range planning effort.
- ☐ Both head and chair should be convinced of the need for a new plan, or nothing will come of it.

## The strategic planning committee

The strategic planning committee makes recommendations on mission, strategies, and policies to the board and monitors the progress of the operating plan. Because planning should involve the largest possible cross section of the school, strategic planning committees usually have between twelve and twenty members: trustees, administrators, faculty members, graduates, parents, and, in upper schools, students. (The committee can become much smaller at the later stage of monitoring the plan's progress.) The planning process may take a few months of intensive work or be spread over a school year. A consultant who specializes in this kind of planning with not-for-profit organizations can be helpful.

The strategic planning committee is often best led by two people— one from the board, the other from the administration or the faculty. While the head and the board chair usually sit on the committee, leadership by others can encourage a fresh look at the institution and its environment.

- ☐ A strategic plan is one prerequisite for an effective major fundraising campaign and for determining what qualities and training are needed when the school is looking for a new head.
- ☐ The people who are going to implement the plan should be involved in designing it. A sense of involvement by faculty members, administrators, and other key people in the school community lowers resistance to change.
- ☐ The planning process itself strengthens the school community by fostering collaboration between constituencies.

## The strategic plan

Strategic planning can be summarized in six steps.

**1.** The strategic planning committee considers the external climate of the institution, listing external changes that might affect the school, such as changes in technology, in educational trends, family structures, tax laws, the local economy, and the condition of local public schools. The committee needs to obtain material on possible future trends, national and local demographic data, economic indicators, and regional and city planning documents.

**2.** The committee considers the internal climate of the school, examining the school's program, the faculty, constituencies, marketing, and governance. The committee needs previous planning and accreditation reports, the mission statement, comparative budget figures from previous years, admission data, and data on faculty turnover, salary scale, faculty-student ratio, and student contact hours.

**3.** Committee members individually define their vision of the institution fifteen to twenty years hence.

**4.** The committee separates into three or four groups to agree on a vision and identify a set of policy goals. These are then presented to the committee as a whole, which decides on final goals and related issues that the board should address.

**5.** The committee appraises the school's mission statement. Is it consonant with the goals the committee has identified? Is it being lived up to? Does it reflect the life of the school? Does it need modification?

**6.** The head of the school, working with the committee's leaders, prepares a report of a dozen pages or less, listing goals and recommendations on mission, policies, and strategies for board consideration.

## The operating plan

Each goal identified in the report of the strategic planning committee needs to be supported by a set of operating objectives and strategies determined by the board. The objectives are then assigned for action to an individual, such as the head, or to a committee. Budget projections can help determine how much time the school may realistically need to meet each goal. The operating plan should include objectives for each area of the school. (See the head's budget preparation, p. 43.)

The operating plan projects conditions for five or more years ahead, but progress should be measured at least yearly. Has the objective or strategy produced the desired result? Is it on schedule? Have enough people been assigned? Enough money budgeted? And, if desired results are not being achieved, what might be changed to bring this about?

# Assessing school performance

Because the board is responsible for the school's mission and educational priorities, it needs to evaluate the school's performance. It reviews programs and policies to make sure that these are consonant with the school's ethos and that they are effective and well managed. As part of this review, the board tries to get a feel for the school—a sense of the spirit and interest of faculty and students.

## The education committee

To assess the school's performance, the board may designate an education, or curriculum, committee. This group should include faculty members and outside educators, whether they are board members or not. If the faculty has a curriculum committee, the education committee works closely with it.

The education committee works with the head and must be careful not to undermine the authority delegated to the head. The committee looks at the performance of the school as a whole and at the effectiveness of particular programs in the light of what the school hopes to accomplish. An education committee does not examine the teaching methods of individual teachers or pass judgment on the competence of individual administrators.

Because of its central role in educational policy making, a standing education committee sometimes becomes *the* committee to be on. If this is a problem, it can be avoided by having differently constituted ad hoc committees to study different parts of the school's programs.

The education committee may be charged with one or more of four duties.

**1.** To assess the school's performance and to review specific programs and policies. In addition to all academic offerings, areas for review can include extracurricular activities and student life.

**2.** To serve as a forum where head and faculty can discuss new programs before presenting them to the board.

**3.** To monitor the administration's implementation of new programs. (A standing planning committee also can take on this responsibility, or the head can give progress reports to the entire board.)

**4.** To inform itself and the board about programs so that the trustees may serve as knowledgeable advocates to the school's constituencies. (All trustees should inform themselves by visiting the school and attending classes at least once a year, as well.)

The following kinds of information may be useful to the board as it tries to arrive at a sense of the school's performance.

☐ The school's most recent evaluation by a state or regional accrediting association.

☐ Graduates' assessments of how well they were prepared, academically and personally, for their subsequent schools. A questionnaire for graduates one and four years out can elicit this information.

☐ The assessments of selected faculty members at schools or colleges that regularly admit graduates of the school.

☐ A comparison between the standing on national tests of those entering and those graduating from the school.

☐ The advice of outside educational consultants.

☐ Visits to similar schools. It is sometimes easier to discover what is unique about one's own school by comparing it with another.

# Managing finances and assets

In managing the school's assets and implementing important aspects of the development program, the board undertakes operational activities as well as policy-making and review responsibilities. As a result, the board or its committees may work closely with administrators other than the head, such as the business manager or development director. These administrators are responsible to the head, not to the board. Trustees carrying out these operational duties should be careful not to circumvent, or be used to circumvent, the head.

## The treasurer and the finance committee

The treasurer (or finance committee chair) and the finance committee are the officer and the committee specifically charged with fulfilling the board's responsibility to ensure the sound financial condition of the school. A finance committee is composed of a few trustees who have experience in this field.

The treasurer and the finance committee may delegate some of the following responsibilities to subcommittees on the audit, on faculty compensation, and on managing the endowment. (See also the head's budgeting responsibilities, p. 43.)

**1.** The finance committee approves the head's proposed budget before it is presented to the board for discussion and approval.

With some boards, tuitions, salaries, benefits, and financial aid are recommended by another committee or subcommittee before the finance committee gives its view on the proposed budget's financial soundness. These boards reason that the educational policies embodied in tuition and salary decisions are so important that the finance committee should not have exclusive authority for them. For the same reason, other boards have all trustees decide these issues.

To help schools evaluate their position and set goals, NAIS sends the head and board chair of each member school annual statistics on member school administrative and faculty salaries, tuitions, enrollment, financial aid, financial operations, and annual giving. In addition, on a fee basis, NAIS offers anonymous comparative statistics on five to thirty institutions of the school's choice.

**2.** In the absence of an executive committee, the finance committee acts with the board chair to review and recommend the head's compensation and benefits to the board.

**3.** The committee reviews the school's monthly comparisons of budget and expenditures prepared by the business manager or an accountant.

**4.** The committee authorizes and reviews a yearly audit of the school's financial condition prepared by certified public accountants.

**5.** The committee regularly reviews the policies under which financial aid (including loans) is granted.

**6.** The committee periodically reviews the school's insurance policies. Policies should reflect realistic liability levels as measured by the school's experience, the experience of other schools, and marketplace conditions. All schools should carry trustees' and officers' liability insurance.

**7.** The committee supervises the school's investments, if any. The board or finance committee (and some boards have an investment committee as a standing committee, as well) decides on asset allocation and makes recommendations on the endowment spending rate. However, endowments are so important to many schools that it is often wise to have a professional firm manage them. Few trustees have the time or expertise to give school investments the attention a professional can.

## The buildings and grounds committee

In many schools, a building and grounds committee is charged with ensuring that the existing physical property is safe, conforms to all codes, and is adequate to the needs of the school. This committee, which works with the head and the business manager to determine priorities in routine maintenance and renovation, should include faculty and staff members.

Extensive new construction or renovation may require design, legal, and management skills beyond the scope of the usual buildings and grounds committee. In this situation, it may be advisable to form a small ad hoc building committee, possibly consisting of the head, the board chair, and a few trustees or members of the school community who have design and construction experience.

This committee may wish to engage architects and contractors other than the ones who usually serve the school. An architect good at designing and carrying out routine maintenance—someone skilled at making do and dealing with the local building department about code compliance—may not have the breadth of vision needed for a master plan. Similarly, the small contractor ideal for summer maintenance work may not have the resources needed for competitive materials procurement or the timely completion of a major job.

- ☐ No matter how small or large the change, the committee should try to include in the design process the teachers, staff members, and students who will be using the space.
- ☐ The committee should designate a single person to speak for the school in all dealings with architects and contractors.
- ☐ In major construction or renovation, it is wise to have someone at the school each day to serve as liaison with the contractors and to note delivery delays, worker absences, and scheduling problems. If the business manager cannot undertake this task, hiring a professional construction manager may save the school money in the long run.

# Development

Fund raising is only the final step in a school's development program. Development, or school advancement, starts with the board's responsibility to the school's constituencies, including the community in which the school is located. In addition to its general responsibility for the school as a public trust, the board has a special accountability to parents, graduates, and donors.

The board—or the head on behalf of the board—should report on its work to these groups at least once a year, giving an account of board actions and decisions, a summary of the operating budget, and, if the school has invested funds, a list of investments.

The development program is intertwined with all aspects of a school's presentation of itself. Each piece of paper the school puts out—correspondence, form letters, brochures, newsletters, press releases—carries a message about the institution. The way the telephone is answered or the school gets in touch with parents can make a difference in enrollment, parental satisfaction, and school fund raising. Development may also include marketing to attract students who might otherwise not consider the school.

## The development committee

Most boards have a development committee that oversees the development program and assumes a leadership role in fund raising. All fund-raising plans for every group—graduates, parents, grandparents, past parents—as formulated by the development office and the head of the school, should be approved by this committee and coordinated by appropriate administrative staff. If the school has a development director, the committee works closely with this person.

The committee regularly reviews the school's publications to ensure that they are consistent with mission and case statements and that all constituencies are being properly informed.

The chair of the development committee should be an experienced trustee. This job is one of the most important—and time-consuming—board positions.

## Fund raising

Schools try to raise two kinds of gifts—annual and capital. Annual gifts are solicited whether a capital campaign is under way or not—and are used to help cover the regular expenses of the institution.

It is wise not to schedule more than three fund-raising events a year for the same constituency. Whatever events are planned (such as an annual fund drive, a benefit, an auction) should be spread throughout the school year.

The dates of development activities should not conflict with other school events, such as parents' meetings, report days, or field days.

The school should hold some events where no fund raising is involved, such as a party or picnic to welcome new families in the fall or to thank the faculty at the end of the school year. Families unable to give must not feel excluded from school functions. All fund-raising functions, such as auctions and fairs, should be designed so that they do not exclude families who have limited resources.

Capital gifts are solicited for special needs, such as financial aid, faculty salaries, a new building, or increased endowment. A capital campaign may ask all constituents for a major gift spread over three to five years or may target parents for a single gift as their children enter or graduate from the school.

For capital campaigns, many schools employ a consultant to conduct a feasibility study to investigate the perceptions of the school's constituencies, to estimate the amount that might be raised, and to help supervise the campaign. A consultant is not needed where the number of prospects is limited or where one or two trustees or a development director know many of the parents and graduates and have the time to help organize other workers.

The head is usually the person who alerts the board to the development needs of the school. The head also states the case for each campaign, meets potential donors, and helps make contact with foundation and corporate executives. Heads of elementary schools rarely solicit parents directly; all families need to feel that they can speak to the head about their children without being embarrassed about not making a gift. Heads of secondary schools generally are expected to solicit gifts from large donors, at least on occasion.

❑ Each trustee should contribute to every school fund-raising effort. Other donors—foundations in particular—look for leadership by the trustees before deciding on a contribution.

❑ Each trustee—not just the members of the development committee —should be prepared to ask other members of the school community to give.

❑ In capital campaigns, most schools expect trustee contributions to equal about a third of the total amount to be raised.

The basic procedures for all fund-raising campaigns—large or small, capital or annual—may be summarized in the following nine steps. The campaign may be managed by a trustee or by the development director, but some board members should be actively involved in either case.

**1.** Compile an accurate record of all past gifts. This is essential for planning present and future fund-raising efforts.

**2.** Identify school needs based on the goals of the strategic plan and a realistic assessment of how much money can be raised in the campaign in question. Goals can be large (increasing faculty salaries or financial aid) or more modest (new library books, gym equipment), depending on the capabilities of the constituencies involved and what other campaigns are planned.

**3.** Document the needs. The document need not be elaborate. It may be only a letter from the board chair accompanying the annual report or a message from the head on an auction invitation.

**4.** Establish a schedule for all parts of the campaign: dates for the completion of brochures, final lists, written committee instructions, committee formation, committee orientation, first mailing, follow-up mailing, individual solicitations, completion of telephone calls, thank you letters.

**5.** Form a campaign committee of trustees and nontrustees to help in soliciting gifts. No committee member should have to ask more than ten others to give, and five is preferable. Large schools may have class committees in addition to the regular development committee and the special committee for that particular campaign.

**6.** Hold an orientation meeting for the campaign committee. At this meeting, the head speaks about the need for the campaign, and the board chair or the development committee chair outlines campaign goals, methods, and schedule; covers points to make in asking for contributions and procedures for referring questions to the head; and asks all committee members to support the campaign generously and early. Committee members receive specific written instructions, a prospect list, record cards to fill out as they complete each solicitation, and the name of someone to call in case of difficulty.

**7.** Record contributions and acknowledge them promptly.

**8.** Call committee members to make sure that they are completing their work on schedule.

**9.** Report interim and final results of the campaign to the school constituencies involved and thank all campaign workers.

## Additional resources

Council for Advancement and Support of Education (CASE), 11 Dupont Circle, Washington DC 20036; (202) 328-5954.

Stone, Susan C. *Strategic Planning for Independent Schools.* Boston: NAIS, 1987.

40

# 4.

# THE BOARD
# AND THE HEAD

The board selects the head of the school and delegates the administration of the school to that person, subject to the board's review. The board works cooperatively with the head to accomplish the school's mission.

The partnership between the board and the head can succeed only through mutual accommodation and trust. Even so, the balance between the responsibilities of the head and the board is sometimes open to legitimate differences of interpretation. For this reason, it makes sense to spell out some of the board's and head's mutual obligations and expectations in a written contract with the head and in a yearly written evaluation of the performance of the head.

## The head's contract

The use of written contracts for school heads has been growing. In 1988, 75 percent of the heads of NAIS member schools had a contract or letter of agreement, as compared to 50 percent in 1979.

A contract provides protection for both parties. Boards change; so do memories of oral agreements. After a few years no trustee may be left from the board that chose the head.

Contracts for new heads generally run for one year. Once the board and the head become better acquainted, an agreement may run for two or three years. A contract usually covers the following four areas.

**1.** The responsibilities of the head and of the board (or a reference to paragraphs in the institution's bylaws that deal with these). Particularly for a new head, the contract may list specific goals to be accomplished within the year.

**2.** Compensation: salary, benefits, and procedures for deciding future compensation; who pays for housing, utilities, insurance, transportation, and school entertaining; any perquisites, such as club memberships, an expense account for school-related travel, professional dues; vacation time; and agreed-upon activities outside the school, such as professional consulting.

**3.** Procedures for evaluating the head's performance: when it takes place, who does it (whether the full board, a committee, or the board chair and selected board officers), whether comments of faculty and administrators are included, how results are communicated to head and board.

**4.** The term of the contract, renewal and termination provisions, what constitutes sufficient notice, compensation in case of termination without sufficient notice.

Both board and head need to know by September if the head will be leaving at the end of the school year. It usually takes about six months for a board to find a new head and for an outgoing head to find acceptable employment, and most school contracts are signed by the end of March, at the latest.

If the board decides to dismiss the head on short notice, the head should receive six months' to a year's salary, with benefits.

# The head's responsibilities

The head serves as the professional educational leader of the institution, administers the school according to the policies set by the board, and works with the board, and particularly with the board chair, to enable the board to carry out its responsibilities.

Within the board's guidelines, the head has complete authority for faculty, staff, and student selection, evaluation, and dismissal. The head has a duty to keep the board informed about all pertinent school matters.

As the professional leader of the institution, the head guides the board in establishing the school's mission and in developing its strategic plan (p. 30), articulates the mission of the school to its constituencies, and is responsible for the professionalism of the faculty.

The head is responsible for implementing the strategic plan by developing annual objectives for all areas of school operations, including

- ☐ Admission, tuition and financial aid
- ☐ Academic course offerings
- ☐ Class size
- ☐ Faculty, administration, and staff: duties, size, salary and benefit scales
- ☐ Buildings and grounds: maintenance, construction
- ☐ Fund raising, endowment

## Preparing the budget

The head's annual objectives are embodied in the budget. Budget proposals are prepared from the bottom up by department and division heads, but the head, assisted by the business manager, is the one who sets the school's priorities (which includes saying no).

The treasurer or the finance committee of the board certifies the soundness of the draft budget. In some schools, another committee (planning, executive, or head's advisory) reviews proposed tuitions, financial aid, and salaries and benefits. Because the budget expresses the educational policy of the school, there is good reason for it to be considered by more than the finance committee.

The budget then is presented to the board for its approval, usually in January. This schedule allows the head to make faculty appointments for the coming year in good time, unless tentative enrollment projections necessitate waiting for a revised budget to make all appointments at the same time. (See the board's management of finances, p. 34).

Once the board has approved the budget, the head, the business manager, and others empowered to spend money should be free to do so within budget limits without having to consult the trustees. For budget control, the head should arrange for the business manager or an accountant to prepare monthly expense figures, with cumulative totals for the year to date compared with the previous year's figures for the same period and the projected budget. The head, board chair, and treasurer can properly expect to see these figures within a few days of the end of each month.

## Reporting

As the administrator of the school under policies set by the board, the head is responsible for and reports to the board concerning all areas of school life. The head also supplies information about the school's enrollment, financial aid program, and salaries to NAIS and its member associations, as part of their regular data-collection activities.

The head regularly furnishes the board with yearly comparative figures about the school's operations. These figures generally form part of the written report the head sends before each board meeting. Topics covered in the course of a year might include

☐ Range of faculty salaries and benefits

☐ Admission applications and acceptances by grade

☐ Ratio of students to faculty by grade

☐ Number of courses and class section sizes

☐ Classroom and laboratory use

☐ Cost per student of student services (athletics, meals)

☐ Fund raising (using figures supplied by the development office)

## Health and safety

The head is responsible for the health and safety of students, administrators, and faculty and staff members while they are under the school's jurisdiction. The head makes sure that the school satisfies the health and safety requirements of state and local authorities.

## Admission and financial aid

The board's admission policy establishes whether the school is coeducational or not, what grades are offered, and how the school deals with applications from siblings or children of graduates, desirable gender balance (in a coeducational school), and minority representation. Within this framework, the board delegates responsibility for admitting students to the head. The head, with the director of admission, has the sole right to decide on student admission as long as decisions are consonant with board policy.

The head should be willing to hear from trustees who can add significant information concerning a family and an applicant, but the final admission decision is the head's. Students, families, and the school are far better served if it is the school's policy to accept children for themselves and not for their families' influence.

The board's financial aid policy establishes criteria and procedures for granting gift aid and loans (which families eventually repay). As with admission, once financial aid policies are established the board delegates authority for these decisions to the head.

- ☐ Over 1,300 schools follow the recommendations of the School and Student Service for Financial Aid, sponsored by NAIS and operated by the Educational Testing Service, which provides a standard data-collection form and method of computation for determining financial need.

- ☐ Aid or loan decisions should be made by someone trained in financial aid procedures and should not be a matter for personal negotiation.

- ☐ The board committee responsible for financial matters should review aid and loan procedures and criteria periodically but should not decide individual cases.

- ☐ Tuition remission or loans granted to faculty children should be determined according to the same criteria used for other applicants for financial aid. A school may decide to give preference to faculty children if financial aid funds are limited.

- ☐ NAIS strongly endorses financial aid on the basis of need rather than merit to increase the diversity of families in the school rather than to attract potential star performers.

## Student discipline and dismissal

The head is responsible for student discipline. The head has the right to dismiss any student who, in the judgment of the head and administrators, should be separated from the school for academic reasons or for unsatisfactory behavior.

The school's philosophy and requirements should be published in a student handbook, along with any specific grounds for suspension and expulsion and the procedures in such cases. These procedures should be reviewed periodically by counsel. The handbook should be discussed in admission interviews and student and parent acceptance of the school's regulations made a condition of admission.

Discipline and dismissal must be based on due process—procedural fairness. Legally, an implied contract may be found to exist between a school and its students. The school obligates itself to provide an education within the terms of its philosophy, established practices, and rules. The students (or their parents for them) obligate themselves to abide by the requirements of the school. Suspension or expulsion may be permitted only after a student has been told of the alleged offense and given a reasonable opportunity to respond. The school should keep written records of all events and procedures in each instance.

❑ In cases of potential student dismissal or suspension a standing faculty or faculty-student committee may make initial recommendations to the head, which the head then may accept or modify.

❑ It is wise for the head to notify the board chair of an impending student or faculty suspension or dismissal. This is not to ask permission but to avoid having the chair and other trustees taken by surprise and to let them know the full facts of the case.

## Faculty selection, evaluation, and dismissal

The head has sole responsibility for the employment of faculty, administrators, and staff members and should not be asked to present alternative candidates for the board's consideration. The head takes responsibility for appointing the best people to be found at levels of compensation within the board's established range, scale, and policy. If the head wishes to create a new position of some importance, such as assistant head, the position and its compensation range should be established with appropriate board officers or committees before interviews with candidates begin.

The board has a right to be informed of median salaries and the range of salaries and benefits but not to know individual salaries, except under exceptional circumstances. The board chair or treasurer (or a finance or a personnel committee) review the extent of all salary changes to assure the board that the policy of advancing teachers on the salary scale is being properly observed. The board in consultation with counsel should review the school's employment policies and procedures periodically to ensure that there is no discrimination on account of sex, race, color, national origin, age, handicap status, or religion in faculty appointments or compensation.

The head, along with the department heads, formally evaluates and makes suggestions for improving the professional performance of the faculty. The head evaluates the performance of department heads and administrators. The board should approve evaluation formats and assure itself that records are kept of all evaluations, but individual evaluations normally are seen only by qualified administrators and the faculty member involved.

The head prepares procedures for faculty dismissal in cases of incompetence, misconduct, change of program, or the need to reduce staff. These should be reviewed by the board in consultation with counsel. In cases of possible faculty misconduct, a committee of faculty members may make initial recommendations to the head, which the head then may accept or modify. If a faculty member has broken the law, the head must notify the appropriate authorities.

## Public relations

The head has the final responsibility for all publicity and all representations to the public made by the school. The head makes sure that the school has written policies concerning sensitive issues such as the presence of AIDS in the school community, nondiscrimination, child abuse, suicide, terrorism, and South African investments.

- ❑ The head is responsible for planning in advance how to respond to a crisis (such as the molestation of a student, a serious accident, a fire). In addition to having procedures for informing and comforting the immediate school community, the school should be prepared to inform its wider constituencies about what has happened and what is being done. The school should designate a single spokesperson and know how to reach legal counsel at all times. A school that is already acquainted with local press, radio, and television reporters on a day-to-day basis will be able to function far better during a crisis than a school that is not.
- ❑ The head is responsible for developing and carrying out a school marketing plan, but the trustees should be a part of it.

## Physical property

The head, working through the business manager, is responsible for seeing to routine maintenance and repair of buildings and grounds. Since head and staff are on the property daily, it is up to them to inform the board's buildings and grounds committee of any unusual conditions. The committee should have both a short- and long-term maintenance program, organized in priority order.

## Legislative and regulatory developments

The head is responsible for seeing that the school keeps abreast of state and federal regulations and that the board is alerted to legislative actions affecting or likely to affect the school. Sometimes a trustee takes on this job at the head's request. State, regional, and local independent school associations and NAIS are good sources of this information.

## Working with the board

Finally, the head works with the board, particularly with the board chair, to enable the board to carry out its responsibilities. The partnership between head and chair is described more fully in the following section, on the responsibilities of the board chair. The head's role in assisting the board is covered there and in these earlier sections.

# Evaluating the head's performance

The head of the school deals with all the individuals and constituencies in the school. As a result, the head moves in an atmosphere of constant approval, criticism, pressure, acceptance, gossip, and informal evaluation. For the board to evaluate the head's performance formally each year makes the head less vulnerable to casual, partisan evaluations and provides a procedure for agreeing on the head's priorities for the coming year.

This evaluation takes place after the board and board chair evaluation, usually in the late spring or early summer. Its findings are kept as separate as possible from decisions about the head's compensation (usually made in January or February, along with faculty and staff compensation decisions), because its purpose is to improve or sustain the work of the head and to set goals.

While most schools devise their own format for evaluating the head's performance, evaluations usually cover

❑ School priorities and the head's goals for the year
❑ The head's communication with the board chair, the board, and the school's constituencies
❑ The head's management and delegation of responsibility within the school
❑ How well the head articulates the school's mission

The evaluation may also include questions about how well the head functions informally within the school and the head's management style.

The group doing the evaluation may be the full board or, occasionally, a board committee. The procedure for evaluating the head's performance is very similar to that for board and board chair evaluation (see p. 25) and can be summarized in the following seven steps. (See the Appendix for a sample head evaluation form.)

**1.** Together the board chair and head, perhaps with some senior trustees or the head's advisory committee, devise an evaluation method and questionnaire. The topics, procedures, and group doing the evaluation must be acceptable to the head (these may be specified in the head's contract). A clear understanding must be reached with regard to anonymity or attribution when questionnaire responses are discussed with the head.

**2.** The board chair sends the questionnaire to each trustee participating in the evaluation (and to faculty members and administrators, if they are involved in any part of it; see p. 29 for discussion of possible faculty involvement in the board and head evaluation process.). As with the board and board chair evaluation, the trustee in charge—the chair—needs to know the name of each respondent to be able to follow up as necessary. Finally, the chair tabulates the responses.

**3.** The head prepares an informal self-evaluation based on the goals of previous evaluations, tasks outlined in the contract, and the school's strategic plan. Comments from administrators or selected faculty members may be included in this self-evaluation.

**4.** The board chair, perhaps with a few other trustees, discusses questionnaire and self-evaluation responses confidentially with the head.

**5.** The chair gives the board a written summary of the board's evaluation of the head along with the head's self-evaluation. This summary is anonymous but should indicate if an opinion is widely held.

**6.** After discussion, the board recommends whatever changes in or reinforcement of the head's goals or methods of management it feels are in the best interest of the school for the coming year. These may be reflected in a letter to the head or simply written into the minutes of the board meeting. In either case, these goals serve as the basis for evaluating the head's performance the following year.

**7.** Board and head review the procedures followed in the evaluation just completed and approve a format for the coming year.

If the head's performance receives serious criticism, the board and board chair should set precise intermediate goals, with a schedule for their accomplishment. (For example, the head might be asked to meet with all department heads individually and to prepare an operating plan for the following year within the next two months, or to hire an accountant and have monthly budget comparisons ready in three months.) Under such circumstances, specific interim evaluations take place every few months, probably with the head's advisory committee in attendance (see p. 66 for the duties of this group).

# The board chair's responsibilities

The chair leads the board, acts in partnership with the head to achieve the mission of the school, and is responsible for working relations between board and head. If possible, the chair should agree to serve for at least three years, for board and head both need this continuity of experience, leadership, and counsel. If the pressure of board work makes this time commitment too burdensome, it may be that trustee terms are too short or that the board meets too often and gets too involved in the administration of the school (see pp. 9 and 19).

As its leader, the chair organizes the board to fulfill its responsibilities to the institution. The chair also serves as a model of trusteeship. Trustees learn from the chair how to understand and respond to school issues.

☐ The chair works closely with the committee on trustees (nominating committee). Thoughtful trustee selection and orientation are essential for an effective board. (See p. 20).

☐ The chair runs board meetings. While realizing that issues need full discussion, the chair should try to forge board consensus. If this proves impossible, even when a decision is held off until a later meeting, it is best to take a decisive vote. Most trustees are content if they feel their views have received fair consideration.

☐ The chair keeps the board and its committees working on schedule.

❑ The chair makes sure that trustees do not become involved in the operation of the school except at the head's request and with the chair's approval.

❑ The chair deals with trustees, or trustees' spouses, who become unduly involved in the day-to-day affairs of the school or who relate board deliberations to those not on the board.

# Board chair and head as partners

Like the board and the head, the chair and the head have separate responsibilities but act as partners. This partnership is a vital factor in the school's well-being. Ideally—and very often, in fact—it is a frank and warm friendship based on the mutual exchange of counsel, criticism, challenge, and commiseration.

Because head and chair are, on different occasions, each the leader and the led, there is bound to be some ambiguity in their functions. Both should try to clarify their roles to their mutual satisfaction. They may disagree on some issues, but they must be able to count on each other's respect and support publicly and privately. They should be able to trust each other to raise potential difficulties well ahead of any board or committee meeting; neither should be the cause of any unpleasant public surprise for the other.

The nature of this partnership will change with time. When the head is new, the chair and the head may wish to meet weekly to discuss problems arising in day-to-day operations. As the head gains experience, it probably is not necessary to meet this often. Still, most heads and chairs bring each other up to date by telephone at least once a week during the school year regardless of how many times they may be together at meetings. Their job in meetings is to forward the work of a group, not to handle matters of concern to them.

❑ Together chair and head identify issues to be addressed and set board agendas. They are jointly responsible for informing the board and the school's constituencies and are both accountable to the board in this role.

❑ They should meet outside the office two or three times a year to talk about long-term issues and dreams.

☐ They should decide, perhaps with an executive committee or a head's advisory committee, who should assume temporary office if the head is suddenly incapacitated. This person might be a senior faculty member or the board chair.

☐ The head should be sensitive to the need of a new board chair for special counsel and support, just as a chair needs to be sensitive to the needs of a new head. New chairs sometimes are not sure how to manage the balance between supporting the head, informing the trustees, and fostering productive board discussion and decision making.

As the person responsible for relations between the board and the head, the chair devises a method of management that complements the head's strengths and compensates for weaknesses. The chair conducts the board's written evaluation of the head's performance and reports the responses to head and board.

☐ Although they work as partners, the chair must be independent of the head in fact and in the eyes of the community.

☐ The head should know in advance about any visits to the school or meetings held by the chair even if these do not involve the head. The chair should not have an office or a desk at the school; this could give the appearance of second guessing or supervising the head. The leadership of the institution is the particular responsibility of the board chair and the head. Both are there to make a difference: to articulate their vision of of how the school's mission can best be carried out, and to persuade others to work toward this end. Every trustee has the right to ask for leadership from the head and from the chair.

☐ Leadership entails not only having a vision but getting others to have it too. This process takes time, but efficiency is not the point; realizing the vision is the point.

☐ A strong chair and a strong head make the best leadership team. If only one is strong, the school suffers in the long run, because there is no person or procedure in place when the strong partner leaves.

# Working with the head

Trustees should remember that the head's job is long and lonely: most heads work more than sixty hours a week during the school year. The head needs the board's informed support, encouragement, and praise privately and in the school community.

- ☐ A head's discretionary fund in the budget for small school projects is welcome.
- ☐ A head's emotional and physical good health is an important priority of the board. Much can be done to foster the head's well-being through provision in the contract for periodic breaks during the school year and at least a month of uninterrupted summer vacation.
- ☐ Heads need to meet with other heads, informally and at conferences and workshops.

The board has a duty to support the head actively and to follow proper procedures in working with the head. If relations between the head and the board are at all troubled, the chair should remind the trustees of these procedures and the need for discretion.

No individual trustee, not even the chair (except when acting on behalf of the board or otherwise as specified in the bylaws), has the authority to give direction to the head. Such authority rests only with the full board in a duly constituted meeting. The board may not give direction to a member of the faculty or administration; that authority rests with the head.

Communication—particularly between the board chair and the head—is vitally important to successful working relations between the head and the board. Some heads may never have attended a board meeting until assuming their present position. Unless the chair tells them, they may not know what is expected in terms of decision making or reporting to the board. Working with the board chair, the head should arrive at a balance that feels right for all parties between too much autonomy (which may surprise and offend trustees) and too much consultation (which may overinvolve trustees in detail and waste their time).

- ☐ Discussion of potential areas of friction ahead of time between the head and the chair can help set guidelines that work best for the school and the people involved.

☐ Board and head evaluations can be used to clarify the decision-making process and to set written goals for board and head for the coming year. The head should be able to ask the board to set these goals.

☐ Using a board committee to study an issue often provides a fresh perspective when head and board are in disagreement and enables them then to find a basis for agreement.

☐ Written reports sent in advance give the board necessary details yet allow time at the board meeting to discuss issues fully. (See the section on board meetings, p. 19.)

☐ Workshops for heads and chairs covering common problems in board-head relations can be beneficial.

☐ A trustee observing something disturbing or problematic at school should call the head. If a trustee speaks directly to the person responsible or involved, this not only circumvents the head but raises the matter to board-level importance, thus compounding the problem raised by the original incident.

☐ A trustee serving as a volunteer in the school (in some capacity other than trustee) is an unpaid employee helping the school, not a trustee visiting the school or making policy.

## Responding to complaints

In the course of their time on the board, trustees of a school hear complaints from parents, students, graduates, and, sometimes, faculty members. Trustees should not try to solve a problem themselves but, after listening, refer the person complaining directly to the head of the school. The trustee should then immediately inform the head of the matter. At all times trustees should be responsive and conciliatory in handling complaints. Silence can be misinterpreted as agreement with a complaint. Sensitive advocacy of the school's position need not be adversarial.

If a complaint comes in writing, any written answer should say that the question is being referred to the head and indicate that a copy of the reply is being sent to the head. If the matter is particularly sticky or serious, or if the person complaining has already spoken to the head, or feels unable to do so, the trustee should mention the matter to the board chair as well, but the head should be informed first and know the name of the person complaining.

An independent school board should not sit as a court of appeal on the head's decisions. A board, or board committee, allowing access to parent, student, or faculty appeal, undermines the authority the board has delegated to the head, inhibits the exercise of the head's best judgment, and makes a clear statement that it questions the judgment of the head—whether or not the head's decision is upheld.

In an extraordinary situation, a board, because it is ultimately responsible by law for the institution, may be required to overrule a head, but this will almost always result in the loss of the head. (See also the board and the faculty, p. 27; student discipline and dismissal, p. 46; and faculty selection, evaluation, and dismissal, p. 46.)

## Board-head problems

When communication breaks down between the head, the board chair, and the board, the institution is in difficulty. A chair who, after trying to work with the head, feels that the head is not informing the board of the condition of the school should document these shortcomings for careful consideration by the full board. The board must then examine its own actions and those of the chair to make sure that responsibilities and procedures have been clearly defined and adhered to. If there is still cause for concern about the head's performance, the board should work with the head to resolve the difficulty. Only if this effort proves unsuccessful over time should the board ask for the head's resignation.

Because the head and the chair are partners, the premature resignation of a head is usually a sad reflection on the performance of the board chair. They succeed or fail together. If chair and head differ too greatly in style to be able to work together, the chair should consider resigning.

When the founder of an institution is its head, the de facto role of the chair and board is mainly one of raising money to support the founder's vision. However, the chair and board may be able to plan for the day when the board will have to institutionalize that vision if the school is to survive.

Sometimes an entrenched chair does not represent the thinking of the board. In this situation, the head, after trying to work with the chair, may ask for a head's advisory committee to discuss and, it is hoped, to resolve the problem. (See p. 66 for other roles for this committee.) The yearly board evaluation, in which the head participates, may also provide an opportunity to address this issue. If a chair is ineffective or if the chair and head together are disregarding the opinions of the board, the committee on trustees should make sure that the annual board and chair evaluation convey an accurate sense of the board's feelings. If necessary, the committee on trustees may recommend a new chair to the board.

# Termination of agreement

The relationship between a school and its head rarely continues until the head reaches retirement age. A board may wish to initiate a change; schools need different kinds of leadership at different times. Heads may feel they have done what they set out to do, they may want a new challenge, or they may wish a more private life and a return to teaching. Nine to fifteen years is the usual period within which a head accomplishes all that one person can as a leader of a particular institution. The advantages of an incumbency of twenty years or more must be weighed against the near certainty of a rough transition period under the eventual new head.

The head and board chair should be able to speak privately to each other about their timetables two or three years in advance. If possible, they should agree not to leave in the same year.

When a change of head is imminent, it is in the interests of the school and the head for notice to be given at least nine, and preferably twelve, months before the end of the school year. Provisions for termination on shorter notice should be detailed in the head's contract (see p. 41). What constitutes reasonable compensation under such circumstances depends on timing (the later in the school year the greater the obligation), length of service, and personal and family circumstances.

☐ The head was chosen by the board and has been the leader of the institution. Sudden dismissal and inadequate compensation do not help the reputation of the board or the school.

☐ Except for reasons of poor physical or mental health, moral turpitude, or serious dereliction of duty, the head should not be required to leave before the end of the school year. Conversely, the head should not leave in the middle of the year, except for a compelling reason of health or a family crisis.

☐ Dismissal action is taken by the full board, not by individuals or committees, and only after the head has been informed of the board's intent, made thoroughly aware of the board's reasons, and given ample opportunity to respond. No individual trustee, even the chair, should try to encourage the head to resign by hinting that such action would be welcome to the board. For ethical and legal reasons, and in the interests of institutional morale and reputation, action to dismiss the head must have integrity. The head should be treated, and be seen to be treated, honorably, and the head's right to due process must be observed.

☐ The board should not start a search or engage a new head without letting the incumbent know. The head is entitled to the earliest possible notice.

☐ The head should not negotiate for another position in secret, telling the board only after having found a new job. On the other hand, the fact that the head may be leaving can disrupt school life, so the the head and board chair may decide to keep this information to themselves until the head is under serious consideration by another institution, at which time the board must be informed.

☐ Once the head has decided to give notice, the school's constituencies should be informed at the earliest possible moment in a statement approved by the head and the board.

In cases of sudden dismissal or succession after a long incumbency, an interim head for a year may be an excellent expedient. An interim headship not only allows time for a proper search but gives the school a chance to make needed changes without burdening a new head with the difficulties involved. NAIS has information about experienced former heads who are available to serve on an interim basis.

❑ Because of the limited tenure of an interim head, it is particularly important for the board and the interim head to have a clear understanding about the interim head's responsibilities in such areas as faculty evaluation, compensation, and reappointment.

❑ If the interim head is a staff member or trustee, it should be stated clearly in advance whether or not that person is a candidate for the head's position.

## Additional resources

*The Audio-Visual Marketing Handbook for Independent Schools.* Boston: NAIS, 1987.

*Business Management for Independent Schools.* Boston: NAIS, 1987.

Dayton, Kenneth N. *Governance Is Governance.* Washington, D.C.: Independent Sector, 1987.

Johnson, Eric W. *Evaluating the Performance of Trustees and School Heads.* Boston: NAIS, 1986.

*The New Marketing Handbook for Independent Schools.* Boston: NAIS, 1987.

Saalfield, Albrecht *A Legal Primer for Independent Schools.* Boston: NAIS, 1983.

# 5.

# A NEW HEAD

**S**electing a new head of school is one of the most important decisions a board makes. For this reason, the search process, which has several distinct phases, must be carefully planned and clearly understood.

## The search process

The search for a new head of school is extremely time-consuming but also extremely rewarding. The search committee gets to know the institution as few trustees ever will and has the privilege of working closely with the administration, faculty, and constituencies of the school.

Because the process is so time-consuming and, often, because they are reluctant to rely on their judgment alone, many search committees turn for help to consultants. Qualified consultants can help define the job and find candidates. They have extensive experience in evaluating resumes and recommendations and can help direct the search process in an orderly, considerate way. Boards should know that consultants are expensive and should be alert to those who might try to impose their own agenda or candidate on the school.

If the search committee decides to use a consultant, the following guidelines apply.

**1.** The school, not the individual candidate, is the consultant's client.

**2.** The consultant should make an effort to learn about and understand the school.

**3.** The consultant should provide a full written description of services offered, including expenses and fees, and a complete list of all schools recently served and client organizations for whom the firm is currently performing a search. The consultant should also indicate which person in the firm will do the search. The committee should interview that person before contracting for services.

**4.** Both the consultant and the search committee should check candidates' references with great care. The search committee has the final responsibility for selection.

## The search committee

Whatever decision is made about using a consultant, the search committee itself should be active throughout the process: define the job, get the word out, screen, interview, and, finally, select the new head.

A search committee usually has between five and eight members— trustees and perhaps graduates or parents. There may be one or two faculty representatives, usually without vote, or a parallel faculty advisory committee that works with the search committee to screen and interview candidates.

A search committee needs secretarial help, an office, a telephone, and a file—often away from the school. It needs a budget for these items and for travel and entertainment. The committee has a demanding schedule of meetings. If possible, the committee should allow six or more months for its work and aim to select a new head by February or March.

The board should approve the search procedures and agree whether final candidates are to be ranked by the search committee or presented to the board for its selection. In either case, the full board makes the final decision.

☐ The current head should not serve on the search committee (which may wish to look for talents different from those of the incumbent). Usually the board chair does not serve on the committee, either.

☐ Often the current board chair agrees to serve for one year after the arrival of the new head in order to smooth the transition. It may be desirable that the person heading the search committee become the next board chair, to work with the new head toward the goals that this person was chosen to reach.

## Defining the job

In deciding what the school wants the new head to do, the search committee re-examines the strategic plan and the school's most recent accreditation evaluation as well as the current head's salary and benefits. The committee drafts a candid statement, for full-board approval, of the school's mission and condition and of what is being sought in a new head. This statement might indicate whether teaching or administrative expertise is more needed or whether leadership potential is more important than extensive academic background.

The search committee and the board should be realistic: the smaller the school, the less likely it is to attract an experienced head, even if an experienced person is what it most needs.

## Getting the word out

Advertisements in educational journals attract applications. So does word of mouth. Parents, graduates, faculty members, and administrators should be asked for recommendations. The present head can ask other heads for suggestions, including possible candidates within their schools. Board chairs of schools that have recently gone through a search can also be very helpful. The NAIS Administrative Clearinghouse and other professional placement services are additional sources of names.

## Screening applications

Applications should be acknowledged upon receipt. If the school is not using a consultant, at least two members of the search committee should go over each candidate's resume, putting aside those obviously not qualified, noting strong candidates, and placing the rest in one or more middle categories.

Those who will not be looked at further should be notified promptly and politely. The others should be told that their candidacies are being actively considered.

Every committee member reads and comments on the applications of highly qualified candidates. Whenever candidates are dropped from consideration they are informed at once.

Candidates' references should be checked before any interviewing takes place. The telephone is convenient and often elicits more forthright evaluations than do written references. Careful notes should be taken on all telephone conversations.

## Interviewing

Small groups of search committee members hold informal preliminary interviews throughout the selection process and report their impressions to the full committee. If they visit a candidate at another school, they should be careful not to jeopardize the relationship of that candidate with the school.

There comes a point when a few strong candidates who have expressed serious interest should come to the school to see and be seen. Candidates should be encouraged to move around the school on their own to get a feel for the place. They should meet formally with members of the search committee, the board chair, other trustees, key administrators and faculty members, the outgoing head (unless special reasons make this undesirable), a group of students, and perhaps with a group of parents or graduates.

- ❑ Throughout the interview process the committee should be sensitive to informal, more personal factors. Do they feel comfortable with the candidate? Could they think of this person as the leader of the school?

- ❑ The committee may ask candidates to provide in advance a short written statement of their educational philosophy or some other topic. It is wise to find out whether candidates can express themselves on paper.

Candor is essential during candidates' visits. The new head will have to deal with the school as it is. If the board plans to alter the established ways of the school, these changes should be carefully explained and their implementation discussed in detail. The candidate should be expected to ask hard questions in return. Lack of board and head clarity in such situations is one reason heads leave or are dismissed after a year or two.

- ❑ Candidates' visits should allow time for informal gatherings as well as formal meetings. An overnight stay with interviews at the school over two days is preferable to a one-day visit.

❏ A preliminary contract discussion should take place at this time.

❏ After they visit, candidates should be told if they are still in the running and asked to say whether they are still interested in the job. They should be told approximately when they can expect to hear the board's decision.

## Candidates' personal situations

In selecting a new head, the school is entering into a relationship not only with the head but with the head's family—whether spouse and children, children from a previous marriage, aging relatives, or partner. The search committee should tell candidates any expectations the school has concerning personal and social values and make clear the extent to which the school can accommodate variations from these expectations.

If the candidate is married, the spouse should be interviewed separately to discuss whether there is interest in a possible social role or other employment at the school, the demands of the spouse's own career, and any other topics or issues needing to be explored.

Many heads need housekeeping arrangements provided and paid for by the school to enable them to function freely. Some schools also pay the head's spouse for performing social duties if the spouse is willing to undertake these.

It is important that all such discussion with candidates and their spouses be nondiscriminatory and otherwise conform to legally mandated hiring practices.

## Final selection

When the list of candidates has been narrowed to two or three, the search committee makes its recommendation to the board. The committee may rank the candidates or ask the board to rank them. The full board makes the ultimate decision, but the search committee's recommendation, if given, is usually accepted. The board should act promptly. Often other schools are considering the same candidates.

❏ The successful candidate and the other finalists should be telephoned at once.

❏ The successful candidate may ask if the choice was unanimous. Trustee reservations may affect the candidate's decision to accept.

☐ The faculty should be informed promptly at a special meeting.

☐ As soon as possible a written announcement should be sent to the school's constituencies, giving an account of the new head's background and experience.

# After the new head takes charge

A new head needs special board support in school and out. Individual trustees, and particularly the board chair, should be ready to adjust to the new head's ways of working and to help the new person settle in and overcome difficulties.

The board should clearly give the new head its confidence and backing. It can take as long as two years for faculty, parents, and students to get used to a change of head. It would be surprising, and unusual, if no group in the school missed the earlier head.

☐ Trustees should introduce the head to the school community and its constituencies. In addition, the executive committee or board officers should see to it that the new head and family are properly introduced to the community at large and encouraged to become a part of it.

☐ The new head should feel free to ask for advice, keep lines of communication open, and not be afraid to ask for help when difficulties occur.

☐ Trustees should be careful to follow proper procedures in responding to questions and complaints (see p. 55).

## The former head

The former head must be careful to stay out of school affairs, to avoid discussions of change in the school, and give advice only when asked to do so by the new head. It is not usually a good idea for the former head to continue to serve on the board or to retain any official connection with the school (such as director of development or of graduate relations).

Retired heads can be extremely effective as informal ambassadors—visiting graduate groups, meeting with major donors to assure them that the school is in good hands—as long as this is done entirely at the behest of the current board and the current head.

## The head's advisory committee

Some schools authorize a head's advisory committee of two or three trustees (not necessarily including the board chair) to counsel the head and to suggest ways of dealing with individuals and constituencies. This committee may be especially useful for a new head who has been charged with making changes in personnel and operating methods.

The advisory committee also may make recommendations concerning the proposed budget (see p. 43) or advise the head when difficulties arise between the head and the board or the head and the board chair (see p. 56). In this latter role, the committee may need to talk with the head or the chair about ways of dealing with people and information that are not working.

While the head has the right to choose the members of the advisory committee, those chosen should be careful not to become, or to seem, a special channel to the head.

If significant changes in personnel or operations are mandated by board policy, the board must be aware of constituent reaction and be prepared to deal with it in full support of the head. Such a unified front is essential if change is to be effected and relatively smooth operation of the institution is to be maintained.

In welcoming a new head and settling that person into the life of the school, good judgment and understanding are needed, as well as good intentions. With these qualities on both sides, the board and head can begin to work together for the betterment of the school.

### Additional resources

NAIS Administrative Clearinghouse. National Association of Independent Schools, 75 Federal Street, Boston MA 02110.

Driscoll, Eileen. *The Selection and Appointment of School Heads.* Boston: NAIS, 1982.

*Principles of Good Practice for Independent School Search Committees and Search Consultants.* Boston: NAIS, 1988.

# POSTSCRIPT

**P**eople make schools, but a school's procedures sustain its people and, through them, the institution as it continually works to educate students and manage change. Procedures reflect and shape the people who develop them; heads and boards have to find their own ways of working to meet their responsibilities to the school and to society.

Throughout, boards and heads have to ask themselves how, together, they can do the best possible job for their school. They must keep steadily in mind what is special about the school—its mission and characteristic spirit—in order to decide on the best possible policies and procedures for the school and for the board. A board's relation to the administration and the faculty is as much an expression of a school's ethos as the education the school offers its students—and will have as great an effect on the institution's future.

The relations between schools, parents, and students, and between school heads, faculties, and boards, will continue to evolve. Boards and heads must consider carefully how these changes may be affecting them. For instance, in the last twenty-five years boards have increasingly looked for and welcomed greater equality in the partnership between the board and the head. The successive editions of this handbook are evidence for this evolution, with its concomitant decrease in the head's authority and growth in that of the board and, to a lesser extent, of the faculty. In consequence, many schools—particularly day schools—are now becoming communities to a degree often not possible before.

In some of these same schools, however, boards still look for a traditional form of hierarchical leadership from the head, even though the current formal and informal organization of the school and the board may mandate that the head lead by acting as a catalyst, by forging coalitions, and by managing consensus. Where disparity exists between a board's expectations for the head and the procedures it has in place to support the head's administration, heads may lose their jobs and schools may lose respect and sense of purpose. A board must make sure that what it wants in a head is congruent with what it wants for the school and for the board's role in the school.

These considerations and the many board responsibilities discussed throughout this book underscore the importance of trusteeship. Independent school trusteeship is a demanding art, but those who have had the privilege of being trustees know that this service has been among the most significant and rewarding acts of their lives. Just as a school is not run for tangible profit and the outcome of an education is largely beyond measure, so the impact of a board on its school cannot be told in numbers. For the same reason, the debt owed by independent schools to the wise governance of their trustees also is beyond measure.

# APPENDIX

## Sample Board, Board Chair, and Head Evaluation Forms

Each board should devise its own forms. Deciding what questions to ask and how to ask them is an important part of the evaluation process. What is appropriate will vary with an institution's size, type, and stage of development and with the board chair's and head's management styles and length of service.

The following sample forms are offered only as guidelines. For more information on the evaluation process and a selection of forms, see Eric W. Johnson, *Evaluating the Performance of Trustees and School Heads* (Boston: NAIS, 1983).

*Board evaluation*

1. What were the board's main goals this year?

2. How well is the board meeting these goals?

3. What should the board's goals be for next year?

4. Is the board a good size?

5. Is the number of meetings satisfactory?

6. Are you comfortable with the mix of committee recommendations and board discussions?

7. What committees are needed—for the present? long-range?

8. What sort of trustees do we lack?

9. Is the written material sent out sufficient to enable you to do your job as trustee?

10. Roughly how many hours a month during this school year did you spend on everything involved with being a trustee?

11. How could your time have been better spent as a trustee?

12. Further comments?

*Board chair evaluation*
(usually a regular part of the board evaluation)

1. What are the immediate and long-term responsibilities of the board chair?

2. How well do you think the chair is fulfilling those responsibilities?

3. Is communication between the chair and the trustees good?

4. Is the chair approachable? Open to new ideas? Can you reach the chair when you need to?

5. Do you think communication between the chair and the head is adequate and effective?

6. Do you think the chair's communication with parents and graduates is adequate and effective?

7. Further comments?

*Head evaluation*
(undertaken by the board and the head after the board and chair evaluations)

1. What were the head's goals for this year?

2. Overall, how well do you think the head has met these goals?

3. Does the head have sufficient staff to do the job properly?

4. Does the head allocate time well? Are there things that aren't getting done? Things the head should stop doing because they don't merit the time spent?

5. Does the head delegate the right amount of authority? Are the lines of authority clear?

6. Is the head able to attract and hold good teachers and administrators?

7. Is the head approachable? Open to new ideas? Can you reach the head when you need to?

8. Does the head know what is going on in the school?

9. Does the head work within the budget?

10. Does the head maintain a good balance between attending to the long-range goals of the school and dealing with immediate problems?

11. Does the head communicate well with all the school's constituencies? How well does the head articulate the mission of the school?

12. What would you say are the head's particular strengths? weaknesses?

13. What should the head concentrate on in the coming year?

14. How can the trustees help the head do the job as well as possible?

15. Further comments?

# INDEX

# About the Author

Barbara Hadley Stanton is a former board chair of The Town School, in New York City (1973-1978), and has served as president of the Independent School Chairmen Association (1978-79), chair of the New York State Trustee Education Committee (1980-81), and chair of the Trustee Committee of the National Association of Independent Schools (1981-1985). Currently she is a board member of a number of local and national educational and service organizations.

She is a graduate of The Brearley School (N.Y.), Vassar College, and Columbia University, from which she holds a M.Sci. in urban planning. Professionally, she conducts research on place cognition and the geographical components of community. She is a member of the Center for Human Environments of the Graduate School and University Center of the City University of New York.